NORTH KOREA: BACK ON THE STATE SPONSOR OF TERRORISM LIST?

HEARING

BEFORE THE

SUBCOMMITTEE ON TERRORISM, NONPROLIFERATION, AND TRADE

OF THE

COMMITTEE ON FOREIGN AFFAIRS
HOUSE OF REPRESENTATIVES

ONE HUNDRED FOURTEENTH CONGRESS

FIRST SESSION

OCTOBER 22, 2015

Serial No. 114–118

Printed for the use of the Committee on Foreign Affairs

Available via the World Wide Web: http://www.foreignaffairs.house.gov/ or http://www.gpo.gov/fdsys/

U.S. GOVERNMENT PUBLISHING OFFICE

97–268PDF   WASHINGTON : 2015

For sale by the Superintendent of Documents, U.S. Government Publishing Office
Internet: bookstore.gpo.gov   Phone: toll free (866) 512–1800; DC area (202) 512–1800
Fax: (202) 512–2104   Mail: Stop IDCC, Washington, DC 20402–0001

COMMITTEE ON FOREIGN AFFAIRS

EDWARD R. ROYCE, California, *Chairman*

CHRISTOPHER H. SMITH, New Jersey
ILEANA ROS-LEHTINEN, Florida
DANA ROHRABACHER, California
STEVE CHABOT, Ohio
JOE WILSON, South Carolina
MICHAEL T. McCAUL, Texas
TED POE, Texas
MATT SALMON, Arizona
DARRELL E. ISSA, California
TOM MARINO, Pennsylvania
JEFF DUNCAN, South Carolina
MO BROOKS, Alabama
PAUL COOK, California
RANDY K. WEBER SR., Texas
SCOTT PERRY, Pennsylvania
RON DeSANTIS, Florida
MARK MEADOWS, North Carolina
TED S. YOHO, Florida
CURT CLAWSON, Florida
SCOTT DesJARLAIS, Tennessee
REID J. RIBBLE, Wisconsin
DAVID A. TROTT, Michigan
LEE M. ZELDIN, New York
DANIEL DONOVAN, New York

ELIOT L. ENGEL, New York
BRAD SHERMAN, California
GREGORY W. MEEKS, New York
ALBIO SIRES, New Jersey
GERALD E. CONNOLLY, Virginia
THEODORE E. DEUTCH, Florida
BRIAN HIGGINS, New York
KAREN BASS, California
WILLIAM KEATING, Massachusetts
DAVID CICILLINE, Rhode Island
ALAN GRAYSON, Florida
AMI BERA, California
ALAN S. LOWENTHAL, California
GRACE MENG, New York
LOIS FRANKEL, Florida
TULSI GABBARD, Hawaii
JOAQUIN CASTRO, Texas
ROBIN L. KELLY, Illinois
BRENDAN F. BOYLE, Pennsylvania

AMY PORTER, *Chief of Staff*   THOMAS SHEEHY, *Staff Director*
JASON STEINBAUM, *Democratic Staff Director*

———

SUBCOMMITTEE ON TERRORISM, NONPROLIFERATION, AND TRADE

TED POE, Texas, *Chairman*

JOE WILSON, South Carolina
DARRELL E. ISSA, California
PAUL COOK, California
SCOTT PERRY, Pennsylvania
REID J. RIBBLE, Wisconsin
LEE M. ZELDIN, New York

WILLIAM KEATING, Massachusetts
BRAD SHERMAN, California
BRIAN HIGGINS, New York
JOAQUIN CASTRO, Texas
ROBIN L. KELLY, Illinois

CONTENTS

NORTH KOREA: BACK ON THE STATE SPONSOR OF TERRORISM LIST?

―――――――

THURSDAY, OCTOBER 22, 2015

House of Representatives,
Subcommittee on Terrorism, Nonproliferation, and Trade,
Committee on Foreign Affairs,
Washington, DC.

The subcommittee met, pursuant to notice, at 2:05 p.m., in room 2255, Rayburn House Office Building, Hon. Ted Poe (chairman of the subcommittee) presiding.

Mr. POE. The subcommittee will come to order.

Without objection, all members may have 5 days to submit statements, questions, and extraneous materials for the record, subject to the limitations in the rules.

In 1987, North Korea bombed Korean Air Flight 858, killing 115 people. For its role in the bombing and its history of other terrorist acts, North Korea was designated as a state sponsor of terrorism from 1988 to 2008.

In 2008, North Korea was taken off the list of state sponsors of terrorism, not because most of the reasons cited in the State Department had changed. Instead, the decision, to me, was purely diplomatic and based on the nuclear agreement reached as a result of the Six-Party Talks. North Korea was to freeze and disable its nuclear program. In exchange, the United States would remove North Korea from the state sponsor of terrorism list.

The agreement fell apart because North Korea did not hold up its end of this bargain. Since 2008, North Korea has made significant advances in its nuclear program. North Korea conducted two nuclear weapons tests since 2008: One in 2009 and one in 2013. Earlier this month, there were rumors of yet another test in the works that may come.

The other reasons the State Department cited for keeping North Korea on the state sponsors of terrorism list for 20 years are still relevant today. North Korea had a long history of abducting Japanese citizens in the 1970s and 1980s. Some of these kidnapped Japanese are still unaccounted for. North Korea has maintained its support for terrorist organizations. North Korea harbored Japanese Red Army terrorists who participated in the hijacking of a jet in 1970. These terrorists are still living peaceably in North Korea today.

In 2009 alone, three North Korean arms shipments bound for terrorist groups like Hezbollah and Hamas were seized by the UAE, Israel, and Thailand. In 2014, Western security sources reported that Hamas brokered an agreement to purchase communications equipment and rockets from North Korea. Hamas fighters reportedly used North Korean anti-tank guided missiles against Israel as recently as 2014.

A U.S. district court ruling in 2014 determined that North Korea materially supported Hezbollah's terrorist attacks in Israel in 2006. And, without objection, the Chair will submit to the record the United States District Court for the District of Columbia, the plaintiffs in cause of action 10–483, where the Federal judge, and I quote, on page 4:

"The court finds by clear and convincing evidence that Hezbollah carried out the rocket attacks that caused plaintiffs' injuries and that North Korea provided material support. North Korea provided Hezbollah with a variety of material support, including a professional military and intelligence training and assistance in building a massive network of underground military installations, tunnels, bunkers, depots, and storage facilities in southern Lebanon."

And it continues. And that will be a part of the record.

North Korea's ties to these terrorists do not end with the weapons sales. North Korean experts advised both Hezbollah and Hamas in the construction of their terrorist tunnel networks.

Beyond its ongoing ties to terrorist groups, North Korea remains a major proliferator of weapons of mass destruction. North Korea has cooperated with Iran on ballistic missiles since in the 1980s. North Korea is now believed to be working on an intercontinental ballistic system. If fully developed, this missile could drop a nuclear bomb as far away as the United States.

There is growing evidence that Iran and North Korea are cooperating on developing nuclear capabilities. North Korea helped set up the nuclear reactor in Syria, which could have been used to produce plutonium for a nuclear weapon. Since 2009, several North Korean shipments of equipment used in chemical weapons programs have been directed to Syria. U.S. Government officials have also said that North Korea provided nuclear material to Libya in the 2000s.

North Korea engages in the harassment, abduction, and murder of refugees, dissidents, and foreigners attempting to help North Koreans defect. The most prominent of these cases is the abduction and murder of Reverend Kim Dong-sik, a U.S. permanent resident from northeastern China.

North Korean cyber attacks have reportedly targeted the Web sites of the Department of Homeland Security, the Department of Defense, Federal Aviation Administration, and others. Last year, North Korea carried out a cyber attack against Sony pictures that included direct threats against its employees and warning to "remember the 11 of September 2001."

Meanwhile, the administration has been exercising a policy of "strategic patience" against North Korea. As a judge, it certainly wouldn't have been good policy for me to have strategic patience for the criminals committing crimes in Texas.

North Korea has not stopped sponsoring terrorism, even if our Government has said it has. The Kim regime not only fails to take substantial steps to combat terrorism, it has provided weapons and other support to designated foreign terrorist organizations.

So North Korea is still manufacturing weapons of mass destruction, and its nuclear program has grown more advanced than in 2008. So it appears that North Korea's actions have gotten bolder and more flagrant. So the purpose of this hearing is to consider putting North Korea back on the state sponsor of terrorism list.

The Chair now yields to the ranking member from Massachusetts, Mr. Keating, for his opening statement.

Mr. KEATING. Well, thank you, Chairman Poe, for conducting this hearing.

And I thank our witnesses for being here today.

North Korea is a rogue state which engages in all sorts of nefarious activities. This is not in dispute. The North Korean regime is involved in international organized crime, perpetrates terrible human rights abuses on its own citizens, and continually engages in internationally provocative actions.

Its nuclear capabilities remain an ever-present threat for its neighbors and for the United States. North Korea has not held back from conducting nuclear tests, engaging in cyber attacks, and ratcheting up military tensions with South Korea. North Korea's continuation of its nuclear and ballistic missile programs is a direct violation of numerous U.N. Security Council resolutions and previously held commitments. Even more disturbing, because of the regime's desperation, its need for hard currency make proliferation and extortion an ongoing threat.

With these violations in mind, I, along with Chairman Poe, cosponsored legislation introduced by Chairman Royce in this Congress to improve the enforcement of sanctions against North Korea. It is important that we, along with our allies, uphold our commitments to North Korea's denuclearization. It is also important that North Korea face consequences when intentionally engaged in prohibited activities.

With respect to North Korea's ties to terrorism, I remain concerned about reports of potential recent North Korean support of Hamas and Hezbollah and reports of attempted and successful kidnappings and assassinations of North Korean dissidents living abroad.

I look forward to hearing from our witnesses regarding these reports and, more generally, how the State Department currently assesses whether North Korea is a state sponsor of terrorism and what factors it considers when making this assessment.

With that, I yield back, Mr. Chairman.

Mr. POE. I thank the gentlemen from Massachusetts.

The Chair will now recognize the gentleman from California, Mr. Sherman, for an opening statement.

Mr. SHERMAN. Thank you.

This hearing raises a number of questions. Clearly, for reasons both prior speakers have indicated, North Korea deserves to be on the list of state sponsors of terrorism. So we will want to know why we took them off, why we haven't put them back on, and why Congress just sits by and lets the executive branch make all the foreign policy decisions, where, in this case, the decision to take them off and leave them off is so questionable.

But then we look at House leadership, which seems to be putting us in a position where the foreign ops bill is going to be presented to Congress in a way in which no member of this committee can offer an amendment. No Member of the House will be able to offer an amendment. And I look forward to working with people here to make sure that just because you stick it in an omnibus bill doesn't mean you can have a whole year or, in this case, several years of foreign ops appropriations with no Member of the House and certainly no member of the Foreign Affairs Committee being able to offer an amendment.

A decade ago, North Korea wanted a nonaggression pact with the United States. We turned them down because we don't do nonaggression pacts, which is perhaps the silliest reason not to do it. Just, ''Well, we don't do that here.'' Now they want a peace treaty. I don't think we should give it to them unless we get something in return, but to dismiss it out of hand seems absurd.

We have taken them off the terrorist list. I don't think we got much for it.

I want to focus our attention on their—we had hearings in this subcommittee with my Asia Subcommittee and others on the North Korea-Iran alliance. I got to spend an hour with the President in the Oval Office. It is amazing how nice the administration is before you announce your position on the Iran deal. And I spent most of that time focusing on the possibility of a transfer of fissile material from North Korea to Iran.

Well, where are we at present? We have one country that desperately wants nuclear weapons and is about to get its hands on, let us say, $100-billion-plus of money. We have another country that has nuclear weapons and fissile material and desperately needs money. What could go wrong? And, certainly, just North Korea's nuclear involvement with Syria and Iran is reason enough to put them on all of the lists.

Israel, roughly 5 years ago, 6 years ago, took out the Al Kibar nuclear facility. The sole purpose of that facility was to help Syrian and/or Iran develop nuclear weapons. At that time, North Korea was unwilling to sell, or apparently unwilling to sell, fissile material because I think they need about a dozen nuclear weapons to defend themselves from us, or at least the speculation is that that is what they think they need. Well, now they will be creating enough fissile material for four additional nuclear weapons every year.

Now, I am not saying their thirteenth weapon goes on eBay, but they have already sold for hundreds of millions of dollars nuclear technology to Syria and/or Syria and Iran. One would suspect more Iran than Syria. And now Iran has a lot more money. And North Korea has more fissile material than it needs as its minimum defense requirement.

So I think we should focus not only on what terrorist and proliferation activities North Korea has engaged in but what they are likely to do in the future.

I thank you for the time, and I yield back.

Mr. POE. Without objection, all the witnesses' prepared statements will be made part of the record. I ask that each witness keep their presentation to no more than 5 minutes. I will introduce each witness and then give time for their statements, and then questions will follow.

Ambassador Kim is the Special Representative for North Korean Policy and the Deputy Assistant Secretary for Korea and Japan. Previously Ambassador Kim served as Special Envoy for the Six-Party Talks and is a former prosecutor.

Mrs. Hilary Batjer Johnson is the Deputy Coordinator for Homeland Security, Screening, and Designations in the Bureau of Counterterrorism. Ms. Johnson oversees the designations of foreign terrorist organizations and individuals under authorities of the Secretary of State.

Ambassador Kim, we will start with you, and you have 5 minutes.

STATEMENT OF THE HONORABLE SUNG KIM, SPECIAL REPRESENTATIVE FOR NORTH KOREA POLICY, U.S. DEPARTMENT OF THE STATE

Mr. KIM. Thank you very much, Mr. Chairman.

Chairman Poe, Ranking Member Keating, and members of the subcommittee, thank you for inviting me today, along with Deputy Coordinator Johnson, to testify about the global security threat posed by North Korea.

North Korea's provocative and repressive policies and actions constitute one of the most difficult and complicated challenges the United States faces. Mr. Chairman, we share your concerns about the grave threat posed by North Korea.

Multiple United Nations Security Council resolutions require North Korea to abandon its nuclear and ballistic missile programs and prohibit countries from engaging with the DPRK to buy or sell weapons and related items and technologies. North Korea itself committed to abandoning all nuclear weapons and existing nuclear programs in the Six-Party process.

Yet North Korea continues to violate these commitments and obligations through its pursuit of nuclear weapons and ballistic missiles and its proliferation of weapons and technologies abroad. This conduct poses a growing threat to the United States, our friends in the region, and the global nonproliferation regime.

We are committed to using the full range of tools—deterrence, diplomacy, and pressure—to counter the threat and to make clear: North Korea will not achieve security or prosperity while the regime pursues nuclear weapons, abuses its own people, and rejects its obligations and commitments.

We have refused to respond to North Korean provocations with concessions. Instead, since 2009, we have tightened sanctions and consistently underscored to the DPRK that the path to a brighter future begins with authentic and credible negotiations that produce concrete denuclearization steps.

Part of our effort to change North Korea's strategic calculus is maintaining the strongest possible deterrent capabilities. The DPRK should have no doubt that the United States stands ready to defend our interests and our allies. In this, we could have no better partners than in our allies in Seoul and Tokyo. We have made it a priority to modernize these alliances for the 21st century, and this important goal was reaffirmed during the recent visits here by President Park and Prime Minister Abe.

By maintaining credible deterrence and by applying sustained sanctions pressure on the regime, we increase the cost to the DPRK of its destructive policy choices. Vigorous sanctions enforcement is the key to cracking down on North Korea's proliferation activities which finance and facilitate North Korea's dangerous programs. Strong sanctions implementation also helps prevent North Korea's weapons from spreading, potentially destabilizing other global hotspots or reaching groups that would seek to harm the United States and our allies.

We of course monitor very closely all available intelligence on North Korea's global arms trade, and we take action, together with our partners, to mitigate those transactions and to impose consequences on those responsible.

In January, President Obama issued a new Executive order giving us an important, powerful, and broad new sanctions tool. We immediately began using this Executive order to apply additional pressure on wrongdoers in the DPRK, imposing sanctions against the DPRK's primary intelligence agency known to be responsible for its cyber operations as well as its main arms trade agency and several of its overseas arms dealers, and we will continue to use this new tool, along with our other sanctions authorities.

Our sanctions are always more effective when supported by our partners, and so we have focused on strengthening multilateral sanctions against North Korea. The sanctions that we have successfully pushed for in the United Nations Security Council give countries the authorities they need to crack down on North Korea's proliferation networks.

When North Korea's major shipping firm was involved in an illegal weapons shipment, we led efforts at the United Nations to sanction the firm. Since then, the company's ships have been denied port entry, scrapped, impounded, or confined to their homeports in North Korea, and the shipping firm has lost its contracts with many foreign-owned ships.

We have engaged countries across Southeast Asia, Africa, and the Middle East that have been targeted by North Korea for proliferation-related activities, reminding them of their obligation to implement United Nations sanctions and strengthening their capacity to do so. As a result of our outreach, key countries have reemphasized their commitment to the United Nations Security Council sanctions and have taken some positive steps on enforcement.

We also continually review all available intelligence to determine whether North Korea is subject to additional measures. Naturally, this includes reviewing available information to determine whether the facts indicate the DPRK should be designated as a state sponsor of terrorism.

Equally important is North Korea's political isolation, driven by the overwhelming international consensus that North Korea cannot fully participate in the international community until it abides by its obligations and commitments. We have built that consensus through our active and principled diplomacy, and that diplomacy, of course, begins with our partners in the Six-Party process: South

Korea, Japan, China, and Russia. Our coordination ensures that, wherever Pyongyang turns, it hears a strong, unwavering message that it must live to up to its obligations.

Mr. Chairman, holding North Korea accountable and combating its illicit activities requires a sustained and international effort. We and our partners will continue to deploy the full range of tools—deterrence, pressure, and diplomacy—to counter the threat and to lead Pyongyang to different choices.

Thank you again for the opportunity to appear today, and I look forward to your questions.

[The prepared statement of Mr. Kim follows:]

**Special Representative for North Korea Policy and
Deputy Assistant Secretary of State Sung Kim**

**Testimony before the House Foreign Affairs Committee
Subcommittee on Terrorism, Nonproliferation, and Trade**

October 22, 2015

Introduction

Chairman Poe, Ranking Member Keating, and members of the subcommittee, thank you for inviting me today, along with my colleague Deputy Coordinator for Counterterrorism Batjer Johnson, to testify about the global security threat posed by North Korea. North Korea's destabilizing, provocative, and repressive policies and actions around the world constitute one of the most difficult and complicated challenges the United States faces. We appreciate the interest and attention you and the subcommittee have given to this issue.

DPRK Behavior

Mr. Chairman, we share your concerns about the grave threat posed by North Korea's illicit weapons programs and its proliferation activities.

Multiple UN Security Council resolutions require North Korea to abandon its nuclear and ballistic missile programs, and prohibit countries from engaging with the DPRK to buy or sell weapons and related items and technologies. North Korea itself committed to abandoning all nuclear weapons and existing nuclear programs in the 2005 Joint Statement of the Six-Party Talks. Yet North Korea continues to violate these obligations and prior commitments through its continued pursuit of nuclear weapons and ballistic missiles, and its illicit proliferation of weapons and technologies abroad. This conduct poses a growing threat to the United States, our friends and allies in the region, and the global nonproliferation regime.

U.S. Policy

We are committed to using the full range of tools – deterrence, diplomacy, and pressure – to counter that threat and to make clear North Korea will not achieve security or prosperity while the regime pursues nuclear weapons, abuses its own people, and flouts its longstanding obligations and commitments.

We have refused to respond to North Korean provocations with concessions. Instead, since 2009 we have tightened sanctions and consistently underscored to the DPRK that the path to a brighter future begins with authentic and credible negotiations that produce concrete denuclearization steps.

Deterrence

Part of our effort to change North Korea's strategic calculus is maintaining the strongest possible deterrent capabilities. The DPRK should have no doubt that the United States stands ready to defend our interests and our allies. In this, we could have no better partners than our allies and friends in Seoul and Tokyo. We have made it a priority to strengthen and modernize these alliances for the 21st Century. This important goal was reaffirmed during the recent visits to Washington by President Park Geun-hye and Prime Minister Abe.

Pressure

By maintaining credible deterrence and by applying sustained sanctions pressure on the regime, both multilaterally and unilaterally, we increase the costs to the DPRK of its destructive policy choices.

Vigorous sanctions enforcement is also the key to cracking down on North Korea's proliferation activities which finance and facilitate North Korea's proscribed nuclear and ballistic missile programs. Strong sanctions implementation also helps prevent North Korea's dangerous weapons and technologies from spreading around the world, potentially destabilizing other global hot spots or reaching groups that would seek to harm the United States and our allies. At the State Department and throughout the U.S. government, we work every day to monitor intelligence on North Korea's global arms trade. And we take action, together with our partners around the world, to mitigate those transactions, and to impose consequences on those responsible.

In January, President Obama issued a new Executive Order giving us an important, powerful, and broad new sanctions tool. From the day it was issued, we began using this Executive Order to apply additional pressure on wrongdoers in the DPRK regime, imposing sanctions against the DPRK's primary intelligence agency known to be responsible for its cyber operations, as well as its main arms trade agency and several of its overseas arms dealers. And we will continue to use this new tool, along with our other sanctions authorities against the DPRK. In July, the Treasury Department released new sanctions designations and updated our listings for previous North Korean sanctions targets to make it harder for them to hide behind aliases and front companies. We are committed to continuing to enforce these sanctions.

But our financial sanctions are always more effective when supported by our partners, and so we've also focused on strengthening multilateral sanctions against North Korea. The sanctions we have successfully pushed for in the UN Security Council give countries around the world the authorities they need to crack down on North Korea's proliferation networks.

When North Korea's major global shipping firm was involved in an illegal weapons shipment, we led efforts at the UN to sanction the firm, and we stepped up coordination with partners to ensure the sanction was enforced. Since then, the company's ships have been denied port entry, scrapped, impounded, or confined to their home ports in North Korea, and the shipping firm has lost its contracts with many foreign-owned ships. This means the DPRK pays a cost for its maritime proliferation.

We have engaged countries across Southeast Asia, Africa, and the Middle East that have been targeted by North Korea for proliferation-related transport and sales, reminding them of their obligation to implement UN sanctions and strengthening their capacity to do so.

Thanks to our outreach – as well as North Korea's continued bad behavior – key countries like China have reemphasized their commitment to UN Security Council sanctions, and have taken some positive steps on enforcement.

We also continually review the available intelligence to determine whether North Korea is subject to additional measures. Naturally, this includes reviewing available information to determine whether the facts indicate the DPRK should be designated as a State Sponsor of Terrorism. Deputy Coordinator Batjer Johnson will speak more about this process.

Diplomacy

Equally important is North Korea's political isolation, driven by the overwhelming international consensus that North Korea cannot fully participate in the international community until it abides by its international obligations and commitments. We have built and maintained that consensus through our active, principled diplomacy.

That diplomacy begins with our partners in the Six-Party Talks: South Korea, Japan, China, and Russia. Our coordination ensures that wherever Pyongyang turns, it hears a strong, unwavering message that it must live up to its international obligations.

At the same time, we have made clear to North Korea that the path of engagement and credible negotiations remains open. Unfortunately, as North Korea continues to reject meaningful engagement, we and our partners must remain focused on enhancing pressure to lead North Korea toward a different choice.

Conclusion

Mr. Chairman, holding North Korea accountable to its commitments and obligations and combatting its proliferation around the world require a sustained, international effort. We and our partners will continue to deploy the full range of tools – deterrence, pressure, and diplomacy – to counter the threat posed by North Korea and to lead Pyongyang to different choices.

I thank the Committee for the opportunity to appear today. I am happy to answer your questions.

Mr. POE. The Chair recognizes Ms. Johnson for your opening statement. You have 5 minutes.

STATEMENT OF MS. HILARY BATJER JOHNSON, DEPUTY CO-ORDINATOR FOR HOMELAND SECURITY, SCREENING, AND DESIGNATIONS, BUREAU OF COUNTERTERRORISM, U.S. DEPARTMENT OF STATE

Ms. JOHNSON. Thank you.

Chairman Poe, Ranking Member Keating, and distinguished members of the subcommittee, thank you for inviting me to join my colleague, Special Representative for North Korea Policy Sung Kim, to testify today about the process for designating a country as a state sponsor of terrorism and North Korea's designation in 1988.

Special Representative Kim already expressed our shared concern for the global security threat posed by North Korea and summarized clearly our policy and tools of deterrence, diplomacy, and pressure. So, with the chairman's permission, I would like to briefly outline the criteria and the process for designating a country as a state sponsor of terrorism ahead of our broader discussions.

First, in order to designate a country as a state sponsor of terrorism, the Secretary of State must determine that the government of such country has repeatedly provided support for acts of international terrorism. The standard for applying and rescinding this designation are set out in the three separate statutes: Section 620A of the Foreign Assistance Act; section 40 of the Arms Export Control Act; and section 6(j) of the Export Administration Act. The standard for designation is the same in all three.

In making such a determination, the Secretary's evaluation generally includes but is not limited to the following criteria. And, I if may, I will read those as well: Allowing the use of its territory as a safe haven from extradition or prosecution for terrorist activity; furnishing arms, explosives, or lethal substances to individuals, groups, or organizations with the likelihood that they will be used in terrorist activities; providing logistical support, such as transportation, to individuals, groups, or organizations involved with terrorist activities; providing safe houses or headquarters for any individuals, groups, or organizations involved with terrorist activities; planning, directing, providing training, or assisting in the execution of terrorist activities; providing direct or indirect financial backing for terrorist activities; and providing direct or indirect diplomatic facilities, such as support or documentation, intended to aid or abet terrorist activities.

A state-sponsor-of-terrorism designation is made only after careful review of all available evidence in its entirety to determine if a country meets the statutory criteria for designation. Such a designation involves a number of laws, and the four main categories of sanctions of an SST would include: A ban on arms-related exports and sales; restrictions over exports of dual-use items; restrictions on foreign assistance; and imposition of miscellaneous trade and other restrictions, including potential liability in U.S. courts for acts that fall within the terrorism exception of the Foreign Sovereign Immunities Act.

The Secretary of State designated North Korea as a state sponsor of terrorism on January 20, 1988, for repeatedly providing support of acts of international terrorism, particularly the bombing of Korean Airlines Flight 858 on November 29, 1987, that killed 115 people and the Rangoon bombing of 1983 that killed 17, including 4 South Korean cabinet ministers.

After a thorough review conducted in accordance with the relevant statutory criteria for SST recision, on October 11, 2008, North Korea's state-sponsor-of-terrorism designation was rescinded.

In May 2015, the United States recertified North Korea as a country not fully cooperating with U.S. counterterrorism efforts, pursuant to Section 40A of the Arms Export and Control Act, as amended. In making this annual determination, the Department of State reviewed North Korea's overall level of cooperation with U.S. efforts to combat terrorism, taking into account U.S. counterterrorism objectives with North Korea and a realistic assessment of North Korea's capabilities.

Of note, the standards are different for certification as a not-fully-cooperating country versus the designation of a state sponsor of terrorism. The determination of whether a country is not fully cooperating is made based on a review of the country's cooperation with U.S. counterterrorism efforts, whereas, again, a state-sponsor-of-terrorism determination is based on whether a country has repeatedly provided support for acts of international terrorism.

In addition to annually reviewing North Korea's certification as a not-fully-cooperating country, the Department of State regularly reviews the available information and intelligence on North Korea to determine whether the facts indicate that it should be, once again, designated as a state sponsor of terrorism. These judgements are not based solely on the news of the day, and we look systematically at what has been done to make these determinations.

In conclusion, I would like to thank you and the subcommittee for the opportunity to appear today along with my colleague, Special Representative Kim, to outline the state-sponsor-of-terrorism process and its history with respect to North Korea, and I am happy to answer any questions.

Thank you.

[The prepared statement of Ms. Johnson follows:]

U.S. Department of State
Deputy Coordinator of Counterterrorism Hillary Batjer Johnson

Testimony before the House Foreign Affairs Committee
Subcommittee on Terrorism, Nonproliferation, and Trade

October 22, 2015

Introduction

Chairman Poe, Ranking Member Keating, and distinguished members of the Subcommittee, thank you for inviting me to join my colleague Special Representative for North Korea Policy Sung Kim to testify today about the process for designating a country as a State Sponsor of Terrorism and North Korea's designation in 1988.

Even without being currently designated as a State Sponsor of Terrorism, North Korea remains among the most heavily sanctioned countries in the world. It is subject to a wide array of layered and severe unilateral sanctions based on its announced nuclear detonations, ballistic missile activity, proliferation activities, human rights violations, and status as a communist state. North Korea has also been sanctioned under multiple UN Security Council resolutions for its ongoing nuclear and ballistic-missile related activities which constitute a clear threat to international peace.

The Process to Designate a State Sponsor of Terrorism

Mr. Chairman, Special Representative Kim already expressed our shared concern for the global security threat posed by North Korea and summarized clearly our policy and tools of deterrence, diplomacy, and pressure.

As requested, today I would like to outline the criteria and process of designating a country as a State Sponsor of Terrorism.

In order to designate a country as a State Sponsor of Terrorism, the Secretary of State must determine that the government of such country has repeatedly provided support for acts of international terrorism.

The standard for applying and rescinding this designation are set out in the three separate statutes: Section 620A of the Foreign Assistance Act (22 USC 2371),

Section 40 of the Arms Export Control Act (22 USC 2780), and Section 6(j) of the Export Administration Act (50 USC app 2405(j)). The standard for designation is the same in all three.

In making such a determination, the Secretary's evaluation generally includes, but is not limited to, the following criteria, consistent with legislative history:

- Allowing the use of its territory as a safe haven from extradition or prosecution for terrorist activity;
- Furnishing arms, explosives, or lethal substances to individuals, groups, or organizations with the likelihood that they will be used in terrorist activities;
- Providing logistical support, such as transportation, to individuals, groups, or organizations involved with terrorist activities;
- Providing safe houses or headquarters for any individuals, groups, or organizations involved with terrorist activities;
- Planning, directing, providing training or assisting in the execution of terrorist activities;
- Providing direct or indirect financial backing for terrorist activities; and
- Providing direct or indirect diplomatic facilities such as support or documentation intended to aid or abet terrorist activities.

A State Sponsor of Terrorism designation is made only after careful review of all available evidence to determine if a country meets the statutory criteria for designation. Such a designation implicates a number of laws; the four main categories of sanctions include:

- A ban on arms-related exports and sales;
- Restrictions over exports of dual use items;
- Restrictions on foreign assistance;
- Imposition of miscellaneous trade and other restrictions, including potential liability in U.S. courts for acts that fall within the "terrorism exception" of the Foreign Sovereign Immunities Act.

North Korea's 1988 Designation as a State Sponsor of Terrorism

The Secretary of State designated North Korea as a State Sponsor of Terrorism on January 20, 1988, for repeatedly providing support to acts of international terrorism, particularly the bombing of Korean Airlines flight 858 on November 29, 1987 that killed 115, and the Rangoon bombing of 1983, that killed 17, including four South Korean cabinet ministers.

After a thorough review conducted in accordance with the relevant statutory criteria, on October 11, 2008, North Korea's State Sponsor of Terrorism designation was rescinded.

North Korea's Certification Status Today

In May 2015, the United States recertified North Korea as a country "not fully cooperating" with U.S. counterterrorism efforts pursuant to Section 40A of the Arms Export and Control Act, as amended. In making this annual determination, the Department of State reviewed North Korea's overall level of cooperation with U.S. efforts to combat terrorism, taking into account U.S. counterterrorism objectives with North Korea and a realistic assessment of North Korea's capabilities.

Of note, the standards are different for certification as a Not Fully Cooperating Country versus designation as a State Sponsor of Terrorism: the determination of whether a country is "not fully cooperating" is made based on a review of the country's cooperation with U.S. counterterrorism efforts whereas a State Sponsor of Terrorism determination is based on whether a country has repeatedly provided support for acts of international terrorism.

In addition to annually reviewing North Korea's certification as a Not Fully Cooperating Country, the Department of State regularly reviews the available information and intelligence on North Korea to determine whether the facts indicate that it should be once again designated as a State Sponsor of Terrorism. As the President said last December, "[W]e don't make those judgments just based on the news of the day; we look systematically at what's been done."

Conclusion

I thank you and the Subcommittee for the opportunity to appear today to outline the process to designate a State Sponsor of Terrorism and its history with respect to North Korea. I am happy to answer your questions.

Mr. POE. Thank you both.

When North Korea was put on the state sponsor of terrorism list, and whatever the reasons were it was put on, which of those no longer apply today in 2015?

Ms. JOHNSON. So, when we rescinded the SST designation, we again go back through the statutory criteria, which require us to go back 6 months that they are listed for the review and determine. And so, at this point, from 2008 on, we, again, review all credible information, all information and intelligence from all sources, and, again, we look to corroborate that, make sure——

Mr. POE. So which of those that were available to you that you said, ''These are the reasons we are putting them on the state sponsor of terrorism''—which of those no longer apply in 2015?

Ms. JOHNSON. Well, I would have to look at what exactly was included in the recision package. But, again, for recision, it is really only a looking back—for the statute requirements—is looking back at 6 months, did they commit any acts of international terrorism. And they also must produce assurances that say they will not commit or provide support for acts of international terrorism going forward. That is the requirement for the SST statute for recision.

Mr. POE. All right.

Ambassador Kim, does North Korea have nuclear weapons?

Mr. KIM. So I think in this setting it is difficult for me to answer clearly, but, obviously, we are very concerned about the advances they have made in their nuclear program.

Mr. POE. Are they developing ICBMs?

Mr. KIM. Well, again, very concerned about the advances they have made in their delivery capabilities.

Mr. POE. And are they working with Iran in the development of ICBMs?

Mr. KIM. So we have long been concerned about relations between Iran and North Korea, and this is a matter that we watch very closely. We have a number of sanctions, both multilateral and U.S. Sanctions, that prohibit any such dealings. And this is obviously something that we will pursue vigorously whenever we have credible information.

Mr. POE. Ambassador and Ms. Johnson, are you familiar with the District Court for the District of Columbia case that I cited earlier, Kaplan v. Hezbollah case? I am sure you have read it. Let me read you another portion that I have not read from the district judge, July 23, 2014:

> ''Moreover, North Korea worked in concert with Iran and Syria to provide rocket and missile components for Hezbollah . . .''

Hezbollah terrorist organization.

> ''North Korea sent these rocket and missile components to Iran, where they assembled and shipped to Hezbollah in Lebanon via Syria. These rocket and missile components were intended by North Korea and Hezbollah to be used and were, in fact, used by Hezbollah to carry out rocket and missile attacks against Israeli civilian targets.''

Now, to me, that sounds like a terrorist act on the end. Would that information be used to consider or reconsider putting North

Korea back on the state sponsor of terrorism list? Either one or both of you.

Ms. JOHNSON. I will go ahead first.

So I wouldn't want to comment on the alleged activities in the district court ruling. Again, I think we—and I believe——

Mr. POE. Well, assume they are true. Just assume that is true. Whether you agree or not, assume it is true. The judge says this, but—I don't want to violate any security things, but assume that is true. Would that be, as we called it in law school, a weight factor to consider putting them back on the list as a state sponsor of terrorism?

Ms. JOHNSON. So, again, I would go back to the statutory criteria requires us to look at all available evidence. We would, again, look at unclassified information, press reporting, other information, including intelligence. And, again, we would be verifying——

Mr. POE. Okay. Excuse me, Ms. Johnson. You read the criteria. I gave you some examples. Would that fit the criteria?

Ms. JOHNSON. Well, I don't want to get into hypotheticals. So, again, you would have to look at a variety of information and sources, again, look if it is, you know, true, credible, corroborated. And you look at it in its entirety.

So I can't speculate, again, on alleged activities and be able to comment——

Mr. POE. Well, that information is disturbing. Would you not agree?

Ms. JOHNSON. A lot of activities in North Korea——

Mr. POE. Mr. Kim?

Mr. KIM. If I may, if true—and I think you are asking us to assume that that report is true, that allegation is true—certainly, it would be a relevant factor for consideration in determining whether North Korea meets the criteria of having repeatedly supported acts of international terrorism.

Mr. POE. All right.

And my understanding is that the policy of the administration in dealing with North Korea is strategic patience. Is that correct?

Mr. KIM. Sir, no. I think the term "strategic patience" was used to describe an approach we were taking to any resumption of negotiations. And the idea was that we wanted to avoid the mistakes that had been made previously with attempts at negotiations with the North Koreans, so we wanted to be more cautious about resuming the negotiations, that we weren't going to rush back to negotiations, that we weren't going to offer any concessions to North Koreans in order to get them to the table.

We wanted to coordinate very closely with our partners. We wanted to deliver to them—we wanted to make sure that we gave us the best chance possible to actually making some lasting concrete progress on the inquisition.

It was not meant to describe our policy. I think our policy is what we both described, which is the combination of deterrence, pressure, sanctions, as well as diplomacy.

Mr. POE. All right. I am out of time.

I will yield to the gentleman from Massachusetts, Mr. Keating, who talks faster than I do.

Mr. KEATING. We both have accents, just different ones.

Again, thank you for being here.

I just want to just dwell on one practical aspect of this. What practical effect would the designation of North Korea as a state sponsor of terrorism have? I mean, they are already heavily sanctioned. There are not many countries more isolated economically in the world than they are.

So, if this occurred, hypothetically, what other added restrictions would be in place? And what would be the effect if it was symbolic? Would that have a practical and an important effect, too?

Ms. JOHNSON. Well, again, if I may, so the SST designation leads to bans on arms-related exports and sales, controls over exports of dual-use items, restrictions on foreign assistance, and other miscellaneous financial and other restrictions.

So when you look at North Korea currently, which is one of the heaviest sanctioned countries around, there is no real practical— I mean, practically speaking, it would not enhance or necessarily alter any of the current sanctions that are applicable to the DPRK at this time.

Mr. KEATING. Yeah. What do you think in terms of a symbol or message that that would make?

Mr. KIM. I mean, I think there is obviously some symbolic value in designating them as a state sponsor of terrorism, but only if they actually meet the criteria for that designation.

If I may, sir, I would just add, I mean, sort of, the flip side of your question is, did they gain anything when we delisted them? And I think the answer is the same. Because, as you pointed out, they are so heavily sanctioned already, both multilaterally and unilaterally, that they really did not gain anything from delisting other than whatever symbolic appreciation they might have had.

Mr. KEATING. Yeah. Just as a process, how does the Department factor in, in this instance North Korea but in any instance, participation in cyber attacks and cyber crime when determining whether it is a designated state sponsor of terrorism?

Ms. JOHNSON. Yeah, and I think, cyber being new, you know, it is an important area.

Mr. KEATING. Yeah.

Ms. JOHNSON. And so we would look at all of that information. And, again, cyber acts is something we would look at. And, again, we would look at the statute, its repeated acts, and, again, if it meets the criteria.

So, again, looking at all intelligence related to a particular cyber attack, we would definitely take a look at it closely.

Mr. KEATING. Yeah.

And, again, getting to the process, as a whole, of the designation, is it—you know, some of the bad acts they are doing and some of the actors they are involved with are actual state sponsors. Can you comment on how the fact that these are state actors, how that might affect the designation process?

Ms. JOHNSON. Well, I mean, it is certainly alarming for us that the DPRK has close relationships with Iran and Syria, both state sponsors of terrorism. But, again, we go back to the legal criteria, and we look at it very closely, of course, because these are state sponsors of terrorism. And we, again, look for repeated acts and, again, verifying and corroborating and making sure credible information exists if there are linkages there, and, again, looking at the relevant criteria.

Mr. KEATING. Yeah.

Now, I know that we are limited, and that is what is a little frustrating in a, you know, open setting. So, to the extent you can—you can follow through in a classified setting, of course—but touching on the support of Hezbollah and Hamas, what would that have as an impact in the designation to any country?

Ms. JOHNSON. And, again, we would be very concerned with any relationships with foreign terrorist organizations and, again, would go back to look at, again, repeated acts. I mean, it sounds very process-oriented, but it is, to make sure that the standard remains the same. Again, are they doing repeated acts or support for acts of international terrorism, and then again looking at the intelligence to see if that backs it up to make——

Mr. KEATING. Yeah. Clearly, would you weigh—it would be much more influential than perhaps state acts, working with state actions of——

Ms. JOHNSON. Yeah, the concern—I mean, very much a concern of state sponsors of terrorism, or STS.

Mr. KEATING. All right.

Well, Mr. Chairman, I will yield back because we are limited in the terms of what we can ask in an open setting along the lines that I was going to pursue. So I yield back my time.

Mr. POE. I thank the gentleman from Massachusetts.

The Chair will yield to the gentleman from California, Colonel Cook, for 5 minutes.

Mr. COOK. Thank you, Mr. Chairman.

I am not an attorney, so I don't understand a lot of the process you are talking about. And I thank my lucky stars.

Ms. JOHNSON. I am not either, if that helps.

Mr. COOK. But the answers you gave there about what you would have to do, I kind of get the feeling that it would take a nuclear event and then it might take 6 months to examine the radioactive material that would be available before you made a decision.

And I am being somewhat caustic, maybe sarcastic, but it almost seems that you are very, very reluctant to establish what line they have to cross that they haven't already crossed. Because I thought they would have met this based upon their past behavior and the terrorist groups that they are associated with.

Ms. JOHNSON. I appreciate the question.

I would definitely say that we take this very seriously, and ''seriously'' means we look, again, at all of the relevant criteria and intelligence and information. And I don't think we want to put countries on the list willy-nilly, so we do a very close examination of all the evidence.

Mr. COOK. Well, it is hard to think of another country that should be closer to the all-star list there, in terms of their behavior.

All right. We will switch gears. I am one of those ones that I think they are just going to thumb their noses at us. But there is one country in the area there that can make a difference and will probably, and that is China. Do you agree with that, that if they were going to change their behavior in a lot of ways, that the fulcrum point is China?

Mr. KIM. Sir, there is no question that China has a special relationship with North Korea, that they have significant leverage over North Korea. And we have urged China to exercise that leverage, use their leverage more effectively to persuade Pyongyang to start making some smart, positive decisions.

Obviously, there is more that the Chinese can do. But I can assure you that they have made very clear publicly, including when Xi Jinping was here just a few weeks ago, that they remain committed to the shared goal of denuclearization and that they strongly oppose any actions by North Korea in violation of Security Council resolutions.

We will continue to work with the Chinese to try to persuade them that they need to be doing more, they need to be doing more effectively, to persuade North Korea back to some credible negotiations, to persuade them to take some concrete actions toward denuclearization.

Mr. COOK. So, officially, the word from China to us is they will not get involved. That is my understanding.

Mr. KIM. Well, I don't think that is accurate, sir. I mean, I think——

Mr. COOK. It is not? You just admitted, you said that they were the one country that probably has the most leverage over that. And they came here and everything, and if we ask them point-blank, the one country there to make a difference, so that they can perhaps save lives or cut down save on this influence, and we don't want to go there? Or am I misunderstanding this?

Mr. KIM. No, sir, I wasn't suggesting that the Chinese are not doing anything or that they are not working with us at all. What we have seen has not been completely satisfactory. And this is why we are continuing to remind the Chinese that North Korea's irresponsible behavior and repressive actions hurt China's own interests, and, therefore, Beijing needs to get more serious, more focused about persuading North Korea.

Mr. COOK. But they haven't done it yet, and they won't do it. Is that correct?

Mr. KIM. I think they are continuing to make an effort, but, obviously, less than satisfactory from our perspective.

Mr. COOK. Effort means a communique to North Korea, ''Hey, knock off the following events. Do this. It is in the best interest of North Korea and China and everyone else to do it.'' Have they done anything? Obviously, I am being allegorical here to a certain extent.

Mr. KIM. I mean, I can tell you that Chinese efforts and sanctions enforcement and implementation have improved over recent years. Is it perfect? No. But we have seen tighter border controls. We have seen stricter controls over export of dual-use items from China to North Korea. So we have seen some improvements, but we need to see more is what I am trying to say.

Mr. COOK. Well, I am running out of time here. I don't agree with you. I don't agree that China has leaned on them at all. And I don't even think they have agreed to the United States that they are going to lean on them. And I think they are the country that probably has the most influence.

And I yield back.

Mr. POE. I thank the gentleman from California.

The Chair now recognizes the other gentleman from California, Mr. Sherman.

Mr. SHERMAN. I think the previous gentleman from California had it right. China is subsidizing North Korea, and China will occasionally send us a statement that says they love us very much and they wish that North Korea wasn't acting so badly.

When we threaten or impose taxes on Chinese exports to the United States, we will get their attention. Until then, we will get statements that I describe as love letters—they may even have little hearts directly from President Xi—saying that they love us very much and they share our goals.

We may need to clarify the state-sponsor-of-terrorism statute because, Ms. Johnson, is there any doubt that—let's say Syria engages is planning terrorism, and they go to North Korea and say, ''Hey, you guys have a special explosive that will help us blow up more people.'' North Korea provides it to Syria. And Syria, not a nonstate actor, Syria itself commits the act of terrorism and kills extra people because they have the good explosives.

Are you saying that, under the statue, it is unclear that that would get a country put on the state sponsor of terrorism list? After all, they didn't help a terrorist group; they didn't carry out an act of terrorism themselves. They just supplied special terrorist equipment to another state sponsor of terrorism.

Ms. JOHNSON. Thank you for the question.

I would say that, again, we look back to the statue, which says repeated acts, that they would provide support for repeated acts of international terrorism.

Mr. SHERMAN. Okay. Let's say they did it four or five times, but all of their aid was to a state actor, not a nonstate actor.

Ms. JOHNSON. So we would look at the intelligence and the available information to be able see——

Mr. SHERMAN. Say it is perfect intelligence; five times, they provided things to Syria that Syria used for terrorism. They are building the barrel bombs.

Ms. JOHNSON. Well, I don't want to get into hypotheticals, but I would say, again, we would look at all——

Mr. SHERMAN. How can I possibly understand how you interpret this statute if we don't get into hypotheticals?

I am asking you a simple question. Is support for a state sponsor of terrorism a reason to put a country on the state sponsor of terrorism list?

Ms. JOHNSON. Again, we would look at——

Mr. SHERMAN. ''We would look at''—can you give me an answer?

Okay. Look, it is pretty obvious you are not following the statute.

Mr. Kim, North Korea abducted Japanese citizens. Are some of them still imprisoned in North Korea, as far as you know?

Mr. KIM. So we don't have that information. In fact——

Mr. SHERMAN. Have they returned the bones, or have they returned the people? All of them. I know they have done on occasion.

Mr. KIM. No.

Mr. SHERMAN. No. Okay. So I would think that kidnapping Japanese citizens is an act of terrorism not only on the day you kidnap them but a month later when you are still holding them, 10 years later when you are still holding them, two decades later when you are still holding them.

Ms. Johnson, I am going to try and understand this 6-month rule. A country is on the state sponsor of terrorism list, but they periodically issue statements saying they don't believe in terrorism. So they have met one of the two prongs. The other prong is they have to go 6 months without engaging in a terrorist act or at least us knowing about it.

Let's say a country meets those two standards. The intel briefs you and says, "It has been 6 months and a day since they have engaged in terrorism that we can document. And, oh, by the way, here is a copy of their most recent statement opposing terrorism."

Under those circumstances, are you saying you can take them off the terrorist list or you are required by law to take them off the terrorist list?

Ms. JOHNSON. So there is nothing under the statute that talks about reviewing. The not-fully-cooperating country list, for instance, there is an annual review, and if you don't recertify, you are off the list.

Mr. SHERMAN. Right. Okay.

Ms. JOHNSON. So, for the statutes, that is not the case. If there is review called, we look back 6 months prior to the call for the review for any acts of international terrorism and for support or——

Mr. SHERMAN. And let's say you look back 6 months and you don't see any. Do you then feel legally compelled to give somebody a get-out-of-jail-free card because it has been 6 months and a day? Or is it just optional with the State Department?

Ms. JOHNSON. Well, we provide the recommendation to the Secretary of State, and then that would go to the——

Mr. SHERMAN. Are you required to recommend that a country be taken off the state sponsor of terrorism list if, as far as you know, they have gone 7 months without blowing anything up?

Ms. JOHNSON. I belive the answer is yes. And I could get back to you on that. But yes.

Mr. SHERMAN. Well, please get back to us. Although, as to North Korea, every day that those Japanese citizens are not returned is a continuing act of terrorism. Every day that the bodies of those who died in North Korea are not returned is a continuing act of terrorism.

So, even if the law is as you describe it, the recommendation of your bureau to take North Korea off the state sponsor of terrorism list was certainly unjustified legally. And then, as far as a matter of politics or international foreign policy, hey, North Korea said it would disable its nuclear installation in Yongbyun, it did, then it didn't, and they are still off the list of—you know. I am not sure that the removal is justified, as a matter of foreign policy.

I yield back.

Mr. POE. The Chair will have another round of questions from the Members of Congress. We will go 2 minutes this time instead of 5.

The Chair will yield to Colonel Cook from California.

Mr. COOK. Thank you, Mr. Chair.

I want to switch gears a little bit. And I understand that the North Korean chamber of commerce and China has probably given them a five-star rating for being good guys, but don't we have the U.S. military that has Top Secret intelligence flying, you know, satellite data, U–2s, and everything else?

And when you talk to the military and if you ask them that question, they would probably say diplomatically, "Not in our area." But then they would tell you things and reasons why you couldn't sleep at night and why the threat is so great, and they would also talk about their affiliation with certain terrorist groups.

Do you guys talk to the military and get that same take that we get, maybe not in Foreign Affairs but the House Armed Services Committee, where we get an analysis of a particular country? And all I have gotten is—boy, if North Korea doesn't qualify for that list, then no one does.

Ms. JOHNSON. Well, we look to the entire intelligence community, and so——

Mr. COOK. But my question, does the military come to you and do you have that exchange that we are having right now? Or is that something outside your realm?

Ms. JOHNSON. No, we are consistently looking at the intelligence and the information. So if military is coming with information, yes, we would——

Mr. COOK. But do you have meetings together where you would have a dialogue like this?

Ms. JOHNSON. We talk to the military intelligence frequently on a number of countries. And, you know, we do have discussions with them regularly, yes.

Mr. KIM. Sir, if I may, I think from our side, as well, we remain in very close touch with our military colleagues.

And I served as U.S. Ambassador to Seoul until just recently, and I know from my own experience that the communication between us, the Embassy, and U.S. Forces Korea continues every day, and it is very much focused on the threat posed by North Korea.

And the same thing in Washington. I stay in very close touch with my colleagues in the Pentagon, and we share information about threats posed by North Korea.

Mr. COOK. Well, as somebody who was in the military a long while, I had a different take on it than you did. So, obviously, my 26 years in the Marine Corps was wasted, because I am very, very worried about North Korea.

I yield back.

Mr. POE. The gentleman yields back.

The Chair recognizes the gentleman from Massachusetts.

Mr. KEATING. Thank you, Mr. Chairman.

I am going to try a thread of questioning that I started and that Mr. Sherman tried to start, and maybe this will yield an answer. Because we are interested in whether the process needs to be altered in any way.

So, in the instance that we both led some questioning on, where it is a state actor that is involved and it is repeated sufficiently and it is credible, would you be precluded from the designation because it is a state actor?

Ms. JOHNSON. If a country meets the criteria and we have the intelligence, again, to support that criteria, we would make a recommendation, yes.

Mr. KEATING. Okay. So you are not precluded by that.

Ms. JOHNSON. But, again, yes, I mean, hypotheticals are hard to answer in——

Mr. KEATING. Oh, I am talking generally, not about North Korea, in this instance.

Ms. JOHNSON. But, again, the criteria, I think, are—I mean, there is no definition of "acts of international terrorism." So we have pulled from the statutes and legislative history and then used——

Mr. KEATING. Right. So the state-actor designation doesn't preclude——

Ms. JOHNSON. So an SST, a foreign terrorist organization——

Mr. KEATING. Right.

And just one other question, because we were talking about sanctions and other issues. And I know this, but I would be interested in Ambassador Kim's comments, you know, that might be more recent or relevant.

They are among the most repressive countries in the world with its own citizens—terrible human rights abuse of its own citizens. How is our intelligence—to the extent that we can talk about this, is there dissent among the people? Is there significant feeling against a country that acts like this? Are there indications that that is increasing recently?

Mr. KIM. Thank you.

I think it is difficult to tell. You would think that there would be dissatisfaction, dissent among the North Korean public, but North Korea remains a unique place. In many bad ways, it is a unique place. The information flow is very limited. The regime remains one of the most brutal. So I think it is difficult for North Korean citizens to express dissent, dissatisfaction in any way that we would be able to detect.

But, certainly, I mean, obviously, we monitor very closely developments on the ground. And we are not seeing any indication of any movement from the North Korean people.

Mr. KEATING. Okay.

I yield back, Mr. Chairman.

Mr. POE. The Chair yields to the gentleman from California, Mr. Sherman.

Mr. SHERMAN. Ms. Johnson, I have, well, a hard question, but it will be easy right now, and that is: I would like you to furnish for the record from your bureau an analysis of how you interpret the law. When are you required to list a state as a state sponsor of terrorism? When are you allowed to do it? When do you have to take them off the list, if ever? When are you allowed to take them off?

And I will ask you to have a series of hypotheticals. If country A—you don't have to name any countries—takes the following action, then we are required to list them, we are allowed to list them, we are required to delist them, we are allowed to delist them.

Because it is our job, when necessary, to rewrite statutes, and if we don't know how you are interpreting this statute, we don't know whether it needs to be rewritten or not. Now, in a perfect world, we would just quickly write a new statue that would be so clear we wouldn't have to ask you how you interpret it. I have learned that Congress is not a perfect world. And if you are interpreting the law in a certain way that seems to be correct, you will save us a lot of time in trying to improve it.

Ambassador Kim, there is a tendency for us to say, "Well, the guys are the bad guys, just do bad things and have no moral compass at all." It has been my experience that bad guys don't think they are the bad guys, and they have their own compass, as distorted—I mean, it may be pointing due south.

And, in looking at North Korea, they seem to be very legalistic, and they seem to care whether we have a nonaggression pact with them—not that that would stop a single division from moving north. They seem to care about whether they are designated as a state sponsor of terrorism, when, in fact, if we took them off the list, that would not improve their economy in any way I can ascertain. And now they are pushing for a peace treaty. And even if we had a peace treaty with them, God knows they engage in activity that would justify unpeaceful activity in the future.

How much do they care about these three things, and why? What is their internal thinking?

Mr. KIM. Thank you very much, Congressman. I think that is a very important question.

Frankly, I am skeptical about their call for a peace treaty because I think they understand that we have certain fundamental requirements. I mean, they would need to denuclearize; they would need to abandon their pursuit of dangerous delivery means, missile capabilities; and they would need to improve their human rights situation. I mean, I cannot imagine any circumstance in which we would enter into a peace treaty with North Korea that continues to reject international obligations and commitments.

So they know that. So for them to be proposing peace treaty negotiations without addressing, sort of, the core issues that we care deeply about, frankly, it is disingenuous. So it is hard for me to, you know, sort of, decipher why Kim Jong-un is so focused on this.

But I agree with you completely that they tend to be very legalistic. And this is, I think, one of the lessons we learned from our previous efforts in negotiating with the North Koreans, is that we really have to be very careful in drafting these documents and entering into any side agreements, because they are very much focused on the most minute details and looking for loopholes wherever possible.

Mr. SHERMAN. Thank you.

Mr. POE. Just a couple more questions. I think we are voting now or soon. Thanks again for both of you being here.

There was a report back in the 2000s, early 2000s, that North Korea set up a nuclear reactor in Syria and then provided nuclear materials to Libya.

Assume that is true. Would that fit the criteria of abetting the proliferation of weapons of mass destruction, which is one of the issues to determine whether somebody should be on the foreign terrorist organization/state sponsor of terrorism list?

Is that right, Ms. Johnson, or not?

Ms. JOHNSON. The FTO list and statutes are different than——

Mr. POE. I know. I meant state sponsor of terrorism. I am not trying to make North Korea a foreign terrorist organization. State sponsor of terrorism is the key here. Would that be a criteria for putting them on the list?

Ms. JOHNSON. Again, I think we look at everything very closely. I know——

Mr. POE. But would it be one of the things that you would look at, this fact?

Ms. JOHNSON. We would look at it very closely and make sure that it is repeated acts for support for international terrorism and, again, evaluate the criteria and look at it holistically and as an entirety. Because, again, I think it is very hard to do hypotheticals without looking at——

Mr. POE. Okay. How about cyber attacks? That was mentioned, but I am not sure I understood the answer. Would that be a new criteria now that you could consider to put a country on the state sponsor of terrorism list?

Ms. JOHNSON. Again, we would review cyber attacks just as closely as any of the other acts. And, again, for cyber attacks, you know, you could look at them in a variety of different ways depending on what we are talking about as far as——

Mr. POE. Yeah. Some of us look at them as an act of war.

Ms. JOHNSON. So, again, we would look at it against the relevant criterial and, again, in its entirety.

Mr. POE. And there are——

Ms. JOHNSON. But repeated acts is an important element.

Mr. POE. Ambassador, I understand there are three countries that are state sponsors of terrorism: Iran, Syria, and Sudan. Is that correct?

Ms. JOHNSON. Yes.

Mr. POE. Is there anybody else that we don't know about?

Ms. JOHNSON. No.

Mr. POE. I mean, that I don't know about.

Kim Jong-un had a press conference, apparently, some time ago. Maybe it was last year. During the press conference, he had behind him a chart or a hit list of things he wanted to destroy. It is kind of personal to me that his first target on that list, with his ICBM capability that he wants, was Austin, Texas. I take that a little personal.

Ms. JOHNSON. Why Austin? Yeah.

Mr. POE. And that was my question. Why Austin, Texas?

But, bigger than that, it seems to me that the government is doing everything it can to be a bad actor in the world. They are helping all the bad guys. They want to be a bad guy. They want nuclear weapons. They want to help sponsor terrorism, Hezbollah, Hamas.

And when I was with the Pacific Command not too long ago, the admiral, I asked him the question: Of the five countries that are threats, or the five entities—China, North Korea, Iran, ISIS, Russia—which one are you the most nervous about? He told me North Korea he was the most concerned about because you never know what they are going to do.

So, anyway, I want to thank both of you for being here. We will have a classified hearing at some later time where we will have more members, and we will have that hearing. Thank you both.

We are voting now, and we are adjourned. Court is over.

[Whereupon, at 3:04 p.m., the subcommittee was adjourned.]

APPENDIX

MATERIAL SUBMITTED FOR THE RECORD

SUBCOMMITTEE HEARING NOTICE
COMMITTEE ON FOREIGN AFFAIRS
U.S. HOUSE OF REPRESENTATIVES
WASHINGTON, DC 20515-6128

Subcommittee on Terrorism, Nonproliferation, and Trade
Ted Poe (R-TX), Chairman

TO: MEMBERS OF THE COMMITTEE ON FOREIGN AFFAIRS

You are respectfully requested to attend an OPEN hearing of the Committee on Foreign Affairs, to be held by the Subcommittee on Terrorism, Nonproliferation, and Trade in Room 2255 of the Rayburn House Office Building (and available live on the Committee website at http://www.ForeignAffairs.house.gov):

DATE: Thursday, October 22, 2015

TIME: 2:00 p.m.

SUBJECT: North Korea: Back on the State Sponsor of Terrorism List?

WITNESSES: The Honorable Sung Kim
                   Special Representative for North Korea Policy
                   U.S. Department of State

                   Ms. Hilary Batjer Johnson
                   Deputy Coordinator for Homeland Security, Screening, and Designations
                   Bureau of Counterterrorism
                   U.S. Department of State

By Direction of the Chairman

The Committee on Foreign Affairs seeks to make its facilities accessible to persons with disabilities. If you are in need of special accommodations, please call 202/225-5021 at least four business days in advance of the event, whenever practicable. Questions with regard to special accommodations in general (including availability of Committee materials in alternative formats and assistive listening devices) may be directed to the Committee.

COMMITTEE ON FOREIGN AFFAIRS

MINUTES OF SUBCOMMITTEE ON _____ *Terrorism Nonproliferation and Trade* _____ HEARING

Day___*Thursday*___Date_____*October 22*_____Room_____*2172*_____

Starting Time ___*2:04 p.m.*___ Ending Time ___*3:02 p.m.*___

Recesses |___| (___to____) (___to____) (___to____) (___to____) (___to____) (___to____)

Presiding Member(s)

Chairman Ted Poe

Check all of the following that apply:

Open Session ☑
Executive (closed) Session ☐
Televised ☑

Electronically Recorded (taped) ☑
Stenographic Record ☑

TITLE OF HEARING:

North Korea: Back on the State Sponsor of Terrorism List?

SUBCOMMITTEE MEMBERS PRESENT:

Reps. Poe, Keating, Sherman, Cook, Castro

NON-SUBCOMMITTEE MEMBERS PRESENT: *(Mark with an * if they are not members of full committee.)*

HEARING WITNESSES: Same as meeting notice attached? Yes ☑ No ☐
(If "no", please list below and include title, agency, department, or organization.)

STATEMENTS FOR THE RECORD: *(List any statements submitted for the record.)*

QFR – Submitted by Rep. Sherman

TIME SCHEDULED TO RECONVENE _____
or
TIME ADJOURNED ___*3:02 p.m.*___

Subcommittee Staff Director

[NOTE: The document submitted for the record by the Honorable Ted Poe, a Representative in Congress from the State of Texas, and chairman, Subcommittee on Terrorism, Nonproliferation, and Trade, entitled, "United States District Court for the District of Columbia: Civil Action No. 10–483 (RCL) and Civil Action No. 09-646 (RCL)," demonstrating a court ruling in 2014 that North Korea materially supported Hezbollah's terrorist attacks in Israel in 2006, is not reprinted here but may be found on the Internet at: http://docs.house.gov/meetings/FA/FA18/20151022/104081/HHRG-114-FA18-20151022-SD001.pdf]

Questions for the Record Submitted to
Deputy Coordinator Hillary Batjer Johnson by
Representative Brad Sherman (#1)
House Foreign Affairs Committee
October 22, 2015

Question:

When it is permissible/required to put a country on the SSOT list?

Answer:

As a matter of law, in order for any country to be designated as a State
Sponsor of Terrorism, the Secretary of State must determine that the
government of that country has repeatedly provided support for acts of
international terrorism. These designations are made after careful review of
all available evidence to determine if a country meets the statutory criteria
for designation. The Secretary of State has considerable discretion in
applying the statutory standard.

Questions for the Record Submitted to
Deputy Coordinator Hillary Batjer Johnson by
Representative Brad Sherman (#2)
House Foreign Affairs Committee
October 22, 2015

Question:

When it is permissible/required to take a country off the SSOT list?

Answer:

There are two possible paths to rescission of a state sponsor designation according to the relevant statutes:

The first path requires the President to submit a report to Congress before the proposed rescission would take effect certifying that:

1. There has been a fundamental change in the leadership and policies of the government of the country concerned,

2. The government is not supporting acts of international terrorism, and

3. The government has provided assurances that it will not support acts of international terrorism in the future.

The second path requires the President to submit a report to Congress, at least 45 days before the proposed rescission would take effect, justifying the rescission and certifying that:

1. The government concerned has not provided any support for international terrorism during the preceding 6-month period, and

2. The government concerned has provided assurances that it will not support acts of international terrorism in the future.

A country's designation as an SST cannot be rescinded until it has met the statutory requirements for rescission.

Questions for the Record Submitted to
Deputy Coordinator Hillary Batjer Johnson by
Representative Brad Sherman (#3)
House Foreign Affairs Committee
October 22, 2015

Question:

If a country gives nuclear weapons or missiles to Iran, Syria or Sudan, will they be put on the SSOT list? Or will that be a criteria considered in determining if a country should be listed?

Answer:

As a matter of law, in order for any country to be designated as a state sponsor of terrorism, the Secretary of State must determine that the government of that country has repeatedly provided support for acts of international terrorism. These designations are made after careful review of all available evidence to determine if a country meets the statutory criteria for designation.

Weapons transfers that violate non-proliferation or missile control regimes could be a relevant factor for consideration, depending on the circumstances, consistent with the statutory criteria for designation as a state sponsor of terrorism.

www.ingramcontent.com/pod-product-compliance
Lightning Source LLC
Chambersburg PA
CBHW081539280526

45788CB00010B/3290